Yoga Sūtra(s)

of Patañjali

in a Nutshell
ILLUSTRATED

Neil Cre

D1502146

ॐ

Yoga Sutra(s) of Patañjali in a Nutshell ILLUSTRATED

N&N Publishing
6369 E Place
McIntosh, FL 32664

352-591-5739

Illustrations by Neil Crenshaw and Ashlynn Price

ISBN 978-1500226640

The OM symbol

Contents

CONTENTS

CONTENTS

Introduction

Being a student of yoga and later a yoga teacher I became interested in learning more about the discipline. I was told by my teacher that a book called the *Yoga Sūtra* is the bible of yoga and if I wanted to really know what yoga was all about I should read it. I got a copy and immediately read it with earnest but I had a difficult time understanding its message. I bought another book on the *Sūtra* but it had a different interpretation which made me somewhat confused. I wondered how two authors could interpret the same thing so differently. I ended up reading five different interpretations of the *Yoga Sūtra* and came away with five different interpretations. This very fact makes the *Sūtra* fascinating reading. My wife, Nancy, who is an English teacher says "All great literature lends itself to varying interpretations." I believe this to be true.

Thousands of years ago storytelling played a big role in passing along history, lore, customs and knowledge from one generation to the next. When Patañjali wrote the *Yoga Sūtra,* about 400 years before the birth of Christ, he took the information that had been orally handed down over many centuries and put it in short, easy to understand verses for those who read Sanskrit.

The original *Sūtra* consisted of a few pages of large script and 196 short verses. Over the past seven hundred years (1400-2015) the *Yoga Sūtra* has been translated into many different languages with many different interpretations. Each author interprets the meaning of Patañjali's teachings differently depending on the author's beliefs, biases about yoga, spirituality, and life in general.

The Sanskrit word *sūtra* can be both pleural and singular. The reason for the (s) on the cover of this book is because most books in English on the *Yoga Sūtra* have an "s" after *Sūtra*. *Sūtras* is a word that has been Anglicized; a foreign word changed for English. I put the *(s)* after Sūtra so when an English speaking person reads the cover they won't be surprised. Also note that the word *Sūtra* has the accent mark "-" above the "u". This means that the "u" is a long "u" and sounds something like "oo" as in *boo*.

Here is verse 20 of chapter II (2:20) of the *Sūtra* similar to what *Patañjali* wrote:

टृटा द्रिसपाक सुद्वाप प्रसापनुपरश

Translated it reads: **draṣṭā drśimātraḥ śuddho api pratyāyanupaśyaḥ.** Here are some possible meanings of these words:

draṣṭā – the seer, perceiver, observer, inner witness

drśimātraḥ – seeing alone, seeing, power of seeing

śuddho – pure

api – very (to express emphasis), even, though, although, but

pratyāya – content of mind, concept, thoughts directed toward an object, the cause, the feeling, notion, presented idea *anupaśyaḥ* – what is perceived, appearing to see, witnessing

Because each interpretation comes from a different author it is possible to have many different versions of the *Sūtra*. You can come away from the readings thinking "Did they read the same original *Yoga Sūtra*?"

What I have done with this book is try to make it as close to what Patañjali wrote - simple and to the point. Here is my interpretation of 2:20 mentioned above, "What the Seer sees is seen though a very pure mind." Simple and to the point with no commentary. But I must add; my interpretation of the *Yoga Sūtra* is by no means all there is to this very important yoga text. When the Hindus read the *Sūtra* 2,600 years ago they understood its meaning in its entirety. They didn't have to have a translation or someone interpret it for them. For Westerners not steeped in Eastern cultures, traditions, and religions it is impossible to not only understand the *Sūtra* completely but difficult to appreciate them for what they truly are, ancient, sacred and enlightened sayings.

The authors of the various interpretations are not to be dismissed. They are Sanskrit scholars and offer their expert interpretations of a very important text. Their interpretations offer much insight and wisdom in the understanding of this ancient text. By reading these interpretations you will understand how difficult it is to convey such writings which say so much in so few words. They have to explain to the Western reader what Patañjali was saying and that is not an easy task.

If you have read some of the other ancient Hindu texts such as *Māhāb*hārata, *Bhāgāvad Gita*, *Upāniṣhad*, and the *Veda* you will be able to understand the *Yoga Sūtra* a little better. Patañjali suggests that you study these sacred texts if you want to progress in yoga. The more you understand Hindu philosophy and religion the more you will be able to understand the art and science of yoga.

In the *Sūtra,* Patañjali doesn't say much about doing yoga postures (*āsana*). In fact, there are only three lines dedicated to doing *āsana.* Patañjali suggests using a posture that is steady and comfortable and to focus on being totally relaxed (2:46-48). It is true that *āsana* are part of yoga, but not the main part. Having said that, however, there is more to asana than just sitting in a comfortable position. Asana can be, and are, used to explore the inner workings of the mind and body. Yoga, taken in its entirety, is an internal as well as in external discipline regarding body, mind, consciousness, and spirit.

It seems that the main theme of the *Sūtra* is to help the aspiring *yogi* reach his ultimate goal of union with the Divine, God, the Absolute principle. The symbol OM represents both the unmanifest and the manifest. The symbol looks something like the number 3 with a tail and a hat (ॐ). The bottom symbolizes the waking state of consciousness which focuses mainly on the senses. The upper curve symbolizes deep sleep without dreaming. The tail represents the dreaming, sleeping state of consciousness. These are the three main states of consciousness: awake, deep sleep, and dreaming. The dot represents the Absolute – the utterly peaceful and blissful state with which the *yogī* aspires to become One. Finally, the slash mark above the "3" represents *maya*. *Maya* separates the dot (Absolute) from who we think we are (consciousness). *Maya* is the illusion that we are separate from God. Once we transcend *maya*, union occurs and we become One with the Absolute.

If you are only doing poses, some breathing exercises, followed by lying in corps pose - *śāvāśana* (shā-vāsh-na), you are not doing traditional yoga as taught by Patañjali. You are doing *āsana*, some *prāṇāyāma*, followed by a rest period. There is nothing wrong with doing yoga poses, breathing exercises and resting. These are good things to do, but you aren't doing true traditional yoga. *Asana* should be interlaced with the other seven limbs of yoga for a balanced and well-rounded practice. The ultimate goal in yoga is to make positive changes in one's life. According to Patañjali you must go beyond the mat and live yoga not for just 90 minutes once or twice a week, but all the time as yoga is a dedication that requires much study and practice.

The word *sūtra* means "thread," as in a suture that a surgeon would use to bring the flesh on either side of a wound together. The *Yoga Sūtra* brings the lessons of yoga together in a coherent understanding of what *yoga* is all about – that of union of subject and object (*samādhi*), spirituality (*sadhāna*), higher consciousness (*vibhūti*), and full liberation (*kaivalya*).

Samādhi Pāda, Sadhāna Pāda, Vibhūti Pāda*,** and ***Kaivālya Pāda are the four chapters of the *Yoga Sūtra*. *Pāda* means to practice. So, the four chapters literally mean to practice union of subject and object, to practice spirituality, to practice higher consciousness, and to practice full liberation. The *Sūtra* provides a thorough and linear way to pursue yoga, and it also clarifies many important concepts related to the philosophical and theoretical art and science of yoga. If it is your intention to do yoga, as it was practiced by the original *yogī*, you may want to follow what is outlined in the *Yoga Sūtra*.

The verses (*sūtra*) are numbered in their particular chapters. I have put some of the verses in groups when they pertain to a common thread while other verses stand alone. In some verses, where deemed important, I have added the translated Sanskrit word after the English word, e.g. in *sutra* 1:16 – true Self (*Purusā*). Although there may be more than one English interpretation of the verses, I have taken what I believe to be the most readily recognized word or words by most English speaking people.

It is hoped that the illustrations which accompany the *sūtra* help to convey its message. I am a visual person and images help me to understand and remember concepts better than almost anything. I did not add commentary to the illustrations because my interpretations would only take away from the reader's own interpretations. I want to leave it up to the reader to come up with his/her own interpretations according to his/her personal background, insight, and impressions.

Patañjali

Drawing from photograph with permission from TOTAL YOGA Bangalore / Pune / Delhi / Singapor

Pronunciations

a   a as in son

a̧   a as in ascent

ā   ah as in father

e   as in bed

é   as a in hay

ḥ   as in half

i   i as in sigh

ī   ee as in see

ṁ   as ng

n   n as in boon

ñ   n as in neighbor

ṇ   as n

ṛ   r as in archer

ś   as in sh

ṣ   s as in almost

t   as in tah

ṭ   as in tea

u   as in full

ū   oo as in hoot

Chapter 1 - Realization Practice (*Samādhi Pāda*)

This chapter discusses the process of yoga and the many, possible, pitfalls one can encounter along the way. The end result is *samādhiḥ* – subject and object become one.

1. The instructions on yoga begin . . . .

2. Yoga is the ability to master the active mind.

3. You will then have stability in the inner self.

4. If you can't control the activities of the mind they will control you.

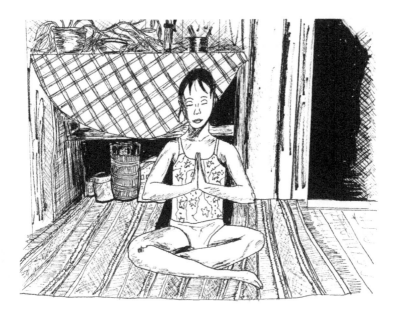

5. Thought patterns are either agonizing and sad (*klișțā*) or non-agonizing and happy (*aklișțā*).

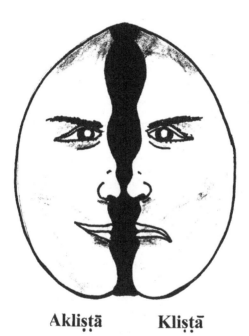

Akliṣṭā   **Kliṣṭā**

6. The mind consists of comprehension, misapprehension, imagination, deep sleep, and memory.

7. Comprehension is knowing the true nature of the object.

8. Misapprehension (confusion) is the inability to understand the true meaning.

9. Imagination occurs without observation.

10. Deep sleep is sleeping without dreaming.

11. Memory is the ability to think of something that happened.

Mind

12. Practice yoga but don't become obsessed with it.

13. Practice, however, is very important.

14. Practice yoga with a positive attitude.

15. Practice yoga and don't become arrogant about it.

16. Practice until you know the true Self (*Puruṣā*).

Practice

17. Practice until you fully comprehend the object you are studying.

18. Practice until there are no longer mental disturbances.

19. If you are born with this ability you don't need to practice yoga.

20. However, if you are not born with this ability keep practicing and have faith.

Keep Practicing

21. If you are faithful to your practice you will attain your goal very soon.

22. Being faithful varies from mild to moderate to intense and not everyone will reach their goal at the same time.

Moderate

Intense

Mild

23. Focus on the Divine (*Īśvara*) and become one with the Divine.

24. The Divine is the All without misapprehension.

25. The Divine is everything. The true Self and the Divine are one.

26. The Divine is eternal.

27. The Divine is represented by the sound "OM."

28. Keep repeating and focusing on the sound "OM."

Iśvara

29. Once you have accomplished total consciousness (*cetanā*), all obstacles will disappear.

30. Understand that there will be many distractions in your practice: illness, lack of focus, doubt, fatigue, pain, frustration, restlessness, thinking, lack of perseverance and foresight.

31. Distractions can slow down and even stop your progress.

32. Continue to stay alert and aware and distractions will not take root.

i COULD

<small>draw a</small> **Picture**

HERE

but it

would

probably

just

distract

you

33. Maintain compassion (*karuṇā*) for all people no matter what their conditions and you will have a clear, peaceful, and calm mind.

Karuṇā

34. Use your breathing with slow exhalation to help you stay focused.

35. Stay alert to all things that may disturb the senses.

Exhale

36. Life itself can cause many distractions.

37. Continue focusing on your goal.

38. Allow the mind to be grounded as in deep, dreamless sleep.

39. And continue concentrating on the object.

40. Once you master this practice the mind will be free.

41. And you will become one with the object.

42. However, the processes of the thinking mind can interfere with this process.

43. With continued focus and concentration, the mind will become clear and union with the object will occur.

44. Your mind may wander and focus on many objects.

45. Bring your focus and concentration back to the object with pure consciousness.

46. Become absorbed and totally one with the object.

47. With this oneness the true Self will become known.

48. At this point total understanding of truth will be revealed.

Union

49. Wisdom gained from within is more significant than that gained from learning or reasoning.

50. Impressions born of this wisdom will surpass all others.

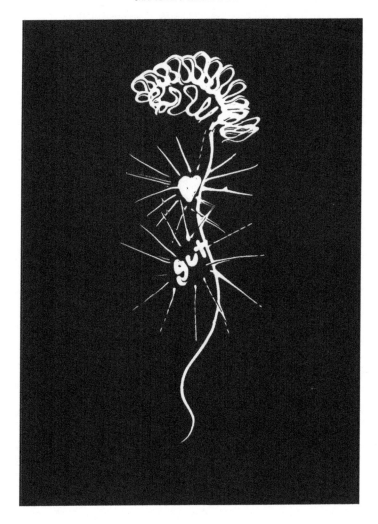

51. The mind has finally become crystal clear and free from any and all distractions. The subject and object merge (*samādhiḥ*).

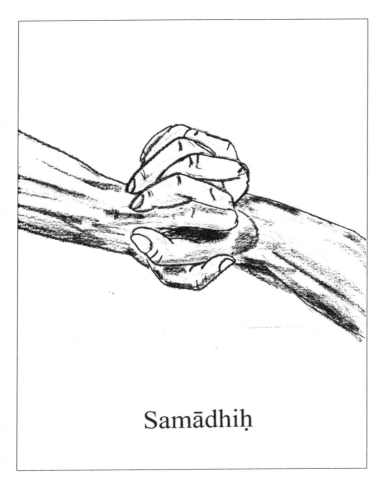

Samādhiḥ

Chapter 2 - Spiritual Practice (*Sādhana Pāda*)

This chapter describes the first five limbs of yoga known as *Ashtānga Yoga*. This is the nuts and bolts of *karma* (cause and effect).

1. The practice of yoga will allow you to become the master of your mind.

2. The practice of yoga will reduce all obstacles and allow your mind to become clear.

Clear Mind

3. The obstacles (*kleśā*) are ignorance, ego, addiction, anger, and fear.

4. Ignorance is the source of all other obstacles no matter whether it is dormant, minimal, active, or at its maximum.

5. Ignorance confuses the temporary with the eternal, the impure with the pure, the self with the true Self, and pain with pleasure.

6. Ego is believing that the mind is the sole source of all perceptions.

7. Addiction is being powerfully attached to a sense of pleasure.

8. Anger is the result of bad and painful memories.

9. Fear is anxiety of not knowing what is to come. It even affects the wisest.

Kleśā

10. When you think you have overcome all obstacles you should become more alert and aware of their presence.

11. The obstacles can be further avoided through meditation practice (*dhyāna*).

12. You should be concerned about the obstacles because they have consequences that may or may not be immediately evident.

13. As long as these obstacles persist they can affect every aspect of your life.

14. The effects may be positive or negative depending on your actions (*karma*).

Obstacle

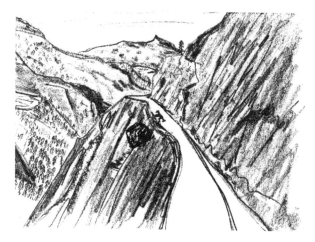

No Obstacle

15. Negative effects are the result of negative actions.

16. Avoid negative actions.

17. Break the bond between the knower – the Seer (*dṛṣṭā*) and what is seen (objects). You should realize that there is a difference between the two.

18. Objects are the mind, the senses, as well as external things (the seen). All three exist for the purpose of experiencing pleasure and illuminating one's knowledge of the true Self.

19. Although these three qualities are different they interact among themselves.

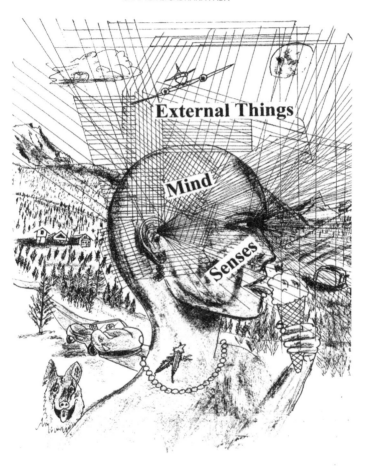

Objects

20. What the Seer sees is seen through a very pure mind.

21. The sole purpose of objects is to be seen by the true Self.

22. Objects exist independent of the needs of the observer.

23. So, they have an effect on the observer but not the true Self.

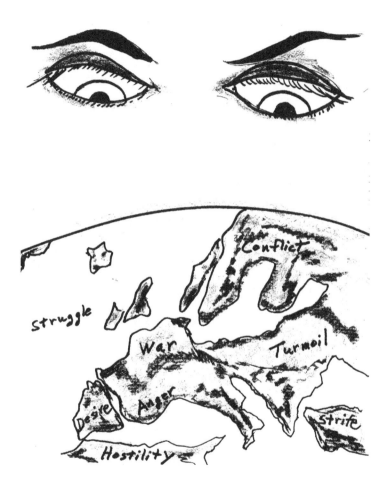

24. The inability to distinguish the Seer from the seen is due to not knowing the true Self.

25. As ignorance decreases clarity increases.

26. Increasing clarity is achieved through acute awareness.

27. There are seven stages you must go through in order to reach ultimate awareness.

28. Sustained practice of these stages will increase clarity between the Seer and the seen.

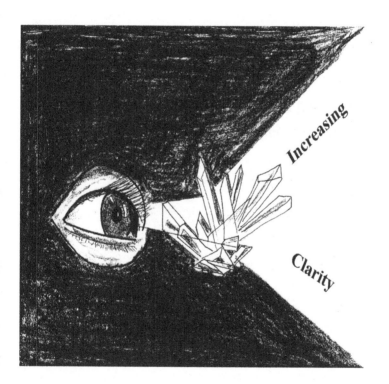

29. The eight limbs of yoga are: *Yama, Niyama, Āsana, Prāṇāyāma, Pratyāhāra, Dhāraṇa, Dhyāna, Samādhi.*

The 8 Limbs of Yoga

30. *Yama* refers to having total self-control, being non-violent, truthful, not stealing, being generous, and always being with the Divine.

31. These are the vows you must take no matter who you are, where you live, your social status, or your intelligence.

32. *Niyama* is cleanliness, contentment, austerity, self-study, and devotion to the Divine (*Īśvara*).

33. When you are in doubt about these attitudes reflect on what the consequences of the alternatives would be.

34. No matter how minor or major the doubt, violence, and anger will always end in suffering. Remember you must always be aware of the alternatives.

Niyama

35. If you are aligned with non-violence (*ahimsā*), hostility will disappear in others.

36. By being honest and truthful (*satya*) your actions will always be fruitful.

37. By being committed to non-stealing (*asteya*), many good treasures will come your way.

38. If you are well established in the awareness of the Divine (*brahmacharya*) you will have great physical and spiritual health (*vīrya*).

39. By being generous (*aparigraha*) you will understand your true nature (*janma*).

40. When your body is clean and your mind is pure you will be content

41. which will make you a pure being with great benevolence linking you to sensual energy, victory, spirit, vision of the true Self (*Ātma darśana*) and fit for doing yoga.

42. From contentment springs great happiness.

43. By eliminating all impurities from the body and mind (*tapas*) you will gain mastery of all your senses.

44. Self-study (*svādhyāyā*) will bring you intimately close to the Divine (*Īśvara*).

45. Meditate, concentrate deeply on *Īśvara* and attain *samādhi.*

46. Use a posture (*āsana*) that is steady and comfortable.

47. Focus your attention on being totally relaxed

48. and you will have freedom from dualities.

Comfortable, Relaxed Posture

49. Control your breathing *(prāṇāyāma)* with slow, smooth inhalations and exhalations.

50. Inhalations and exhalations are both followed by suspended breathing. Focus on making these three components long and smooth.

51. Go beyond your inhalations and exhalations and expand your consciousness.

52. The veil that covers the light will diminish.

Prānāyāma

53. Concentration (*dhāraṇā*) prepares the mind.

Concentrate

54. When you draw your senses inward (*pratyāhāra*) and are no longer focusing on any object, the mind becomes a field of consciousness (*cittasya*).

55. Then you will have ultimate mastery of the senses.

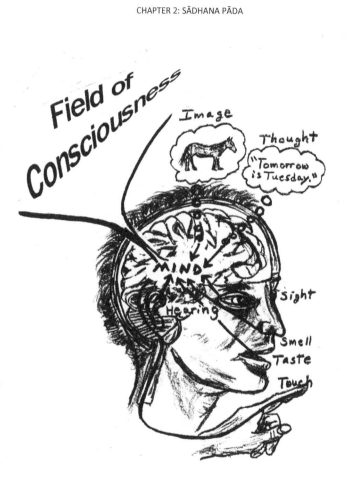

Pratyāhāra

Chapter 3 – Going Beyond Earthbound Consciousness (*Vibhūti Pāda*)

The last three limbs of yoga: concentration, meditation, and *samādhi* are described in this chapter. Together these three limbs are called *saṁyamā. Saṁyamā* can bring great powers but the warning is to not get attached to them for they can be a roadblock to the main goal; that of reaching pure consciousness.

1. Concentration (*dhāraṇā*) is holding your mind on one object.

2. Meditation (*dhyāna*) is continuing to hold the mind therein.

3. *Samādhi* is when you have perfected meditation. The self has emptied and the true essence of your being is all that remains.

4. *Saṁyamā* is all three limbs together.

5. Once you have mastered all three, a higher, infinite consciousness is available.

6. The practice should be done slowly and at your own pace.

7. These three limbs (*dhāraṇa, dhyāna, samādhi*) are more internal than the previous five limbs (*yama, niyama, āsana, prāṇāyāma, pratyāhāra*)

8. but external compared to the highest level of them all.

9. The highest level, *saṁyāma,* can appear in an instant and then disappear because of old habits.

10. But you can override old habits and master the highest level with continuous practice.

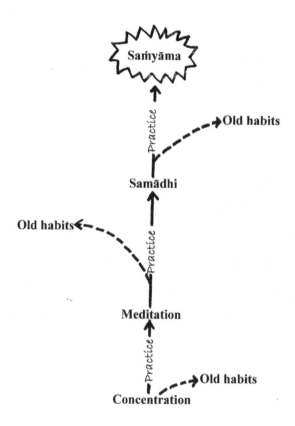

11. *Samādhi* will transform the scattered mind into one that is one-pointed

12. and then those rising and falling thoughts will subside and become highly focused.

13. The material elements of form, time, and condition interpreted by the mind and the senses (*indriya*) will be transformed.

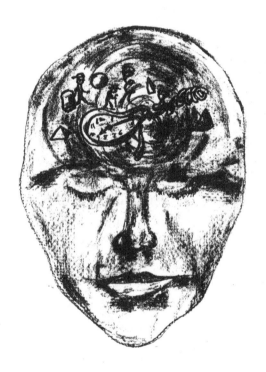

Transformation

14. The qualities among all forms are the same (*Everything is made out of the same stuff*).

15. It even appears that things become different with time.

16. *Saṁyamā* will allow you to understand the three material elements the way they will be in the future as well as the way they were in the past.

17. *Saṁyamā* will give you knowledge about the differences between objects, the meaning of concepts, habits, and speech differences between all living beings.

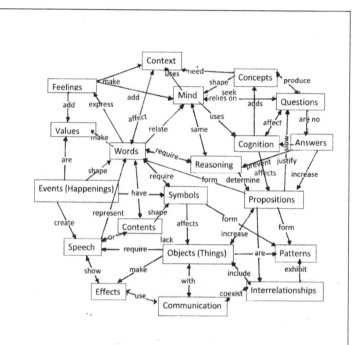

Knowledge

18. By understanding your unconscious mind and deepest habits you can get in touch with your past.

19. With this ability, even the thoughts of others can be perceived.

20. But even so it is still difficult to know the true nature of other people.

Thoughts

21. Concentration, meditation, and *samādhi* (*saṁyamā*) on the material body will suspend the energy from visible light and render the form invisible.

22. This explains why sound from the material body is not heard.

Invisible

23. Your *karma* (life's actions) is occurring now as well as in the future, so the practice of *saṁyamā* on karma will allow you to know the time of your passing.

Know the time of your passing

24. Being friendly will give you strength.

25. Strength like an elephant's strength.

Strength

26. Focusing on the inner light will lift the veil giving you better knowledge.

27. *Saṁyamā* on the inner sun will give you knowledge of the universe,

28. knowledge of the moon and star systems,

29. and knowledge of their movement around the Polar Star.

Inner Light

30. *Saṁyamū* on the navel *chakra* gives knowledge of the body systems.

Navel Chakra

31. By practicing *saṁyamā* on the pit of the throat, hunger and thirst will cease.

Throat Chakra

32. *Saṁyamā* on the upper chest allows you to remain calm and steady.

Upper Chest

33. *Saṁyamā* on the crown of the head and divine light will give you visions of the spiritual masters.

Crown of the Head

34. A flash of intuitive light can give you higher knowledge.

Intuit Power

35. But, by practicing *saṁyamā* on the heart you can have full knowledge.

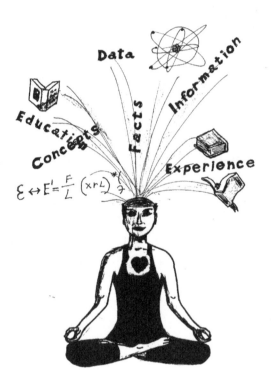

Heart

36. Pure consciousness and the mind are closely related but are separate entities. The mind has concepts and experiences, pure consciousness does not. When they come together you will experience the true Self

37. and then gain spiritual illumination, divine hearing, touch, vision, taste, and smell.

38. But these special abilities of *samādhi* may be obstacles to the highest state.

39. By letting go of those special abilities you may move into another body – the mind-field (*cittasya*)

40. By mastering the upward flow of the life force (*prāṇa*) using *prāṇāyāma* you can rise above destructive forces such as water, mud, thorns, etc.

41. By mastering the flow of vital energy (*samāna*) in the navel area you can create glowing radiance.

42. By practicing *saṁyamā* on your ears and sound in space you can develop divine power of hearing.

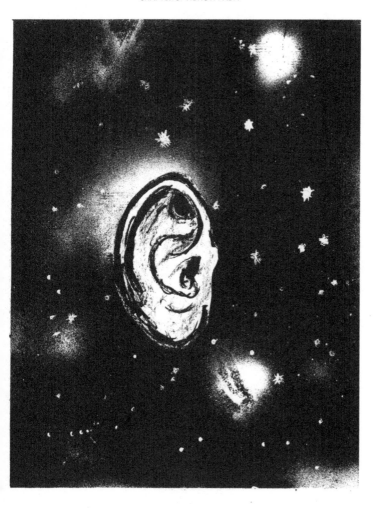

43. Practicing *saṁyamā* on the body and the vastness of space (*ākāsha*) you can become as light as cotton and move freely through space.

44. When your mind is focused on the formless (*mahā-videhā*) the veil that covers spiritual light (*prakāśā*) is removed.

45. Through *saṁyamā* on the five elements (earth, fire, water, air, space) you can gain mastery (*jayaḥ*) over them.

46. With this mastery you will gain quantum powers beyond the body and become perfectly indestructible.

47. This perfect form will have extraordinary abilities, strength, and resilience.

48. Practice of *saṁyamā* yields mastery over the self, the mind, and the senses *(indriya)*.

49. This mastery gives freedom from physical senses faster than thought.

50. You will then understand with clarity the difference between pure mind and true Self (*Puruṣā*) and this will bring complete knowledge, omnipotence, and supremacy.

51. And yet you will not gain absolute freedom
(*kaivalya*) until you lose all attachment to those
powers.

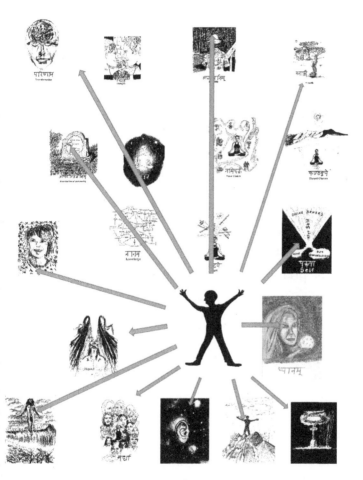

Release all of your attachments to these powers.

52. Don't even accept invitations from spiritual beings because pride can revive unwanted material desires.

53. Knowledge of *saṁyamā* gives you discernment over moments as they pass in time.

54. It also allows you to distinguish the difference between two objects, in all respects, that appear similar.

55. Therefore, complete knowledge is born of discernment of all objects, in all ways, under all conditions, and in any sequence.

56. In the end, *kaivalya* occurs when the purest aspect of the mind becomes equal to pure consciousness.

Chapter 4 – Union of Mind with Pure Consciousness *(*Kaivalya Pāda*)*.

This chapter discusses the aspects of absolute freedom (*kaivalya*).

The mind has many obstacles (colorings) which will try to prevent you from reaching absolute freedom. Perfecting mental abilities, rebirth, and immortality are useless methods for doing so. According to Patañjali the only way to reach absolute freedom is to rid yourself from the power and dominance of the mind and unite the mind with pure consciousness.

1. Perfected mental abilities may be attained by being born that way or by taking special herbs, chanting mantras, training the senses (*tapas*), and intently concentrating on a higher power (*samādhi*).

2. These practices may transform you into another birth (*jātyantara*).

3. But, incidental and indirect causes do not bring about realization. Realization is brought about by removing obstacles much like a farmer removing a barrier allowing water to flow and nourish his field.

4. The ego (*asmitā*), or the I-ness, is what primarily produces thoughts from the mind (*chittā*).

5. Many diverse activities come from the mind.

6. Meditation (*Dhyāna*) frees those thoughts and activities from cause and effect (*karma*).

7. The actions of a *yogī* are steady but for others they are threefold (good, bad, or mixed).

8. The actions of others will be expressed according to their deep impressions (*vāsanānām*).

9. Because memory and deep impressions are similar in appearance, they are similar in their actions even though they are distinctly separate in time, place, and status.

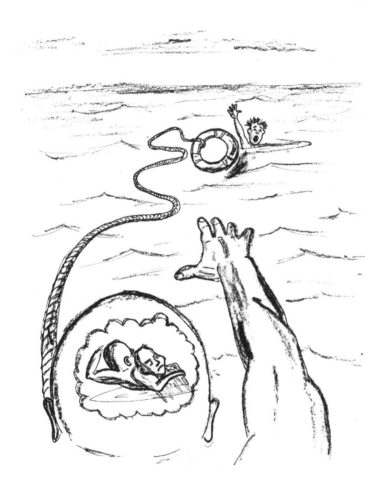

10. Since these memories and impressions (*samskāra*) are timeless, it is ridiculous to desire immortality.

11. They are held together by causes, motives, concepts, and objects. When these obstacles dissolve so will *samskāra*.

12. Past and future characteristics appear different but in actuality they exist entirely in the present moment.

13. Whether the characteristics are manifested or not, they are composed of the forces of nature (*guṇā*) - illumination, stability, and motion.

14. Characteristics of objects appear to change but in essence they remain constant.

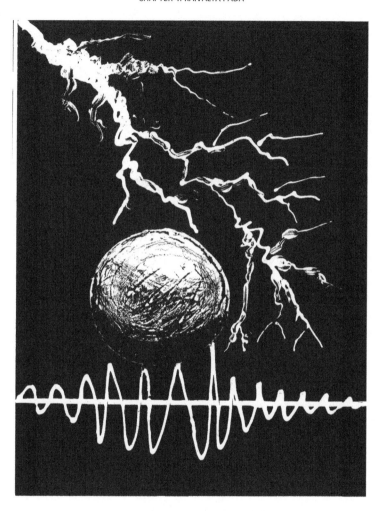

15. Objects are seen differently because the minds of observers are different.

16. The object's existence does not depend on being recognized. Would the object exist if it was not perceived?

17. An object is either known or not known depending on the mental obstacles (colorings) of the mind.

18. Pure consciousness (*Puruṣasyā*) is unchanging and superior to the mind and is always aware of the fluctuations of the mind.

19. The mind is not self-illuminating. Pure consciousness is the illuminator.

20. The mind and pure consciousness cannot be comprehended at the same time.

21. If the mind was able to know what its master was thinking there would be endless confusion.

22. But when the mind sees the master, the mind is transformed into the unchanging Self.

23. So, although the mind has mental obstacles (colorings) it can still have awareness of itself (the seen, the Seer, and all objects). *Note: This is the unfolding of self-realization.*

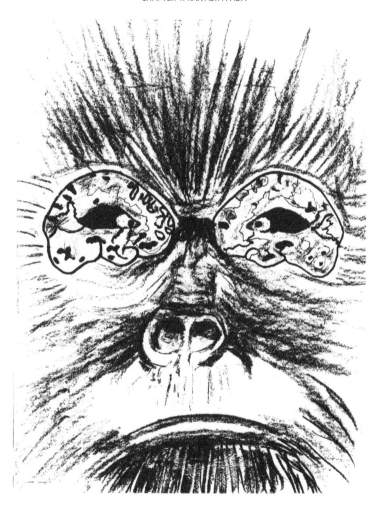

24. Although the mind has accumulated countless desires it exists solely for the purpose of acting closely with the true Self.

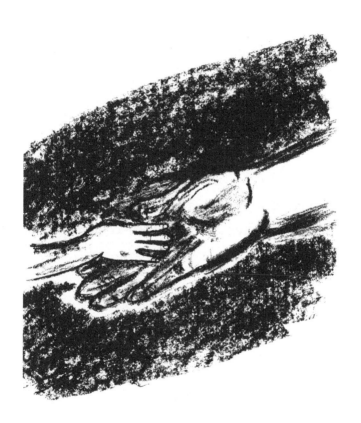

25. When you know the difference between the Seer and the self, cultivating a sense of self-centeredness ceases.

Self-Centeredness

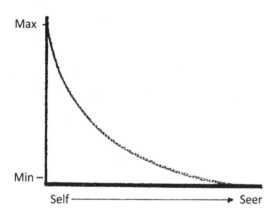

26. Then with greater awareness of the differences between self and Seer you will gravitate toward absolute freedom (*kaivalya*).

27. Due to old habits (*samskāra*), however, there can be thoughts and obstacles causing gaps to appear in the freedom.

28. These obstacles may be removed much like what was done for the five *kleśās* (2.3 – 2.14).

29. Stay in *samādhi* and you will no longer have an interest in a higher consciousness and discernment (discrimination) will be constant. Virtuous rains will pour down upon you.

30. Soon the obstacles (*kleśa*) and bad karma will leave.

31. Then all veils of imperfections will be removed and infinite wisdom will seem trivial.

32. The primal forces (*gunā*), having fulfilled their purpose and no longer needed, will depart the scene.

33. Time seems to be an uninterrupted series of events, but in the end the truth is known.

34. Now that the primal forces recede, the dominant forces of the mind come to an end and absolute freedom (*kaivalya*) is established.

Glossary

Addiction   Being strongly attached to a sense of pleasure.

Ahimsā   Non-violence. One of the 5 *Yama*.

Ākāsha   Vastness of space, cosmos, universe.

Aklistā   Non-agonizing thought patterns.

Anger   The result of bad and painful memories.

Āsana   Yoga posture. One of the 8 limbs of *Ashtanga Yoga*.

Ashtanga Yoga   8-limbed yoga (*yama, niyama, āsana, prānāyāma, pratyāhāra, dhārana, dhyāna, samādhi*).

Asmitā   Ego, I-ness.

Aparigraha   The act of being generous. One of the 5 *Yama.*

Asteya   Non-stealing. One of the 5 *Yama*.

Ātma-darśana   Vision of the true Self.

Ātman   The inner self, soul.

Brahmacharya   To be established in the awareness of the Divine. One of the 5 *Yama.*

Cetanā   Consciousness

Chakra   The energy centers of the body of which there are 7: base of spine, navel area, solar plexus, heart, throat, forehead, crown of the head.

Chittā   The mind, psyche.

Cittasaya   The field of consciousness, mind field.

Colorings   Mental obstacles.

Comprehension   Knowing the true nature of an object.

Deep sleep   Sleeping without dreaming.

Dhāraṇā   Concentration. One of the 8 limbs of *Ashtanga Yoga.*

Dhyāna   Meditation practice. One of the 8 limbs of *Ashtanga Yoga.*

Dṛṣṭā   The Seer – the one who is watching without becoming emotionally involved – the true Self, the Knower.

Ego   Believing that the mind is the sole source of all perceptions.

Fear   Anxiety of not knowing what is to come.

Guṇā   Primal forces of nature: *rajas* - energy, motion, activity, *sattva* - light, luminosity, purity, *tamas* - inertia, stability, heaviness, resistance to action.

Ignorance Confusing the temporary with the eternal, the impure with the pure, the self with the true Self, and pain with pleasure.

Imagination Conjuring up a thought or image in the mind without observation.

Indriya The 5 senses.

Iśvara The Divine, the Supreme Being, God.

Janma Birth, incarnation, true nature.

Jayaḥ Mastery, conquest.

Jātyantara Born again, into another birth.

Kaivalya Absolute freedom.

Karma Law of cause and effect.

Karuṇā Compassion.

Kleśā Obstacles: ignorance, ego, addiction, anger, and fear.

Klistā Agonizing thought patterns.

Knower That which is not affected by the mind, senses, or objects. Also known as the Seer and the true Self.

Mahā-videhā Mind focused on the formless.

Memory Thinking of something that happened.

Mind   Consists of comprehension, misapprehension, imagination, deep sleep, and memory.

Misapprehension   The inability to understand the true meaning (confusion).

Namasté   A salutation meaning "I honor the Divine within you."

Niyama   One of the 8 limbs of *Ashtanga Yoga* – cleanliness, contentment, austere, self study, and devotion to the Divine.

Objects   The mind, the senses, and external things (the seen)

observer   The small self.

Obstacles   Ignorance, ego, addiction, anger, and fear. Colorings.

Pāda   Practice.

Prakāśā   Spiritual light, illumination.

Prāṇa   The life force.

Prāṇāyāma   Control of the life force (*prāṇa*) by using the breath.   One of the 8 limbs of *Ashtanga Yoga*.

Pratyāhāra   Drawing the senses inward.   One of the 8 limbs of *Ashtanga Yoga*.

Purusā   The true Self, pure consciousness.

Pure consciousness   A clear and purified mind devoid of all intrusive thoughts.

Realization   Enlightenment, knowing the true Self.

Sādhana   Spiritual.

Samādhi   Spiritual union of the subject with the object. The 8th and last limb of *Ashtanga Yoga.*

Samāna   Equilizing *prāna* around the navel air using *prāṇāyāma.*

Samskāra   Latent or subliminal impressions, habits.

Saṁyamā   The combined practices of concentration (*dhāranā*), meditation (*dhyāna*), and samādhi.

Satya   Honesty and truthfulness. One of the 5 *Yama.*

seen   External objects.

Seer   That which is not affected by the mind, senses, or objects. Also known as the true Self, the Knower.

Self   That which is not affected by the mind, the body, the senses, or objects. Also known as the Seer and the Knower.

self   That which is identified with the mind, the body, and the senses.

Svādhyāyā   Self-study, study of the psyche.

Tapas   The energy or passion, "heat," you put into your practice of yoga.

Vāsanānām   Deep impressions, subconscious tendencies.

Vibhūti   Going beyond earthbound consciousness, transcendence.

Virya   Having great spiritual and physical health.

Yama   One of the 8 limbs of *Ashtanga Yoga.* Having total self-control, being non-violent, truthful, not stealing, generous, and being with the Divine.

Yoga   Being absorbed in God, *Iśvara*, the Supreme, The Divine, the Absolute, the All.

Yogī   One who does yoga.

References

Beloved, Michael. *Yoga Sūtras of Patanjali*, 2007.

BonGiovanni, translator. *The Yoga Sutras of Patanjali, The Threads of Union*, www.sacred-texts.com.

Chalam, Majoj. *Spiritual Art and Mythology of India, Anecdotes & Symbolisms*, San Diego, CA: Unique Arts International, no date.

Desikachar, TKV. *Reflections on Yoga Sūtra-s of Patañjali*, Chennai, India: Yoga Mandiram, 2003, Reprinted 2008.

Forstater, Mark and Manuel, Jo. *Yoga Masters, How Yoga Theory can Deepen Your Practice and Meditation*, New York, NY: Plume, 2002.

Jnaneshvara, Swami. *Traditional Yoga and Meditation of the Himalayan Masters, Self-Realization through the Yoga Sutras, Vendata, Samaya Sri Vidya Tanra.* www.swamij.com/yoga-sutras.

Madhavananda, Swami, Translated and Annotated by. *Vendānta Paribhāsā of Dharmarāja Adhvarīndra,* Kolkata, India: Advaita Ashrama, April 2004.

Maki, Bhāvani Silvia. *The Yogī's Roadmap, The Patañjali Yoga Sutra as a Journey to Self Realization,* Hanaleik Kauai, HI: Viveka Press, 2013.

Sanskrit Script Writing – Learn Languages. Mylanguages.org/sanskrit_write.php. 2011,

Shearer, Alistair, Translated and Introduced by. *The Yoga Sutras of Patanjali,* New York, NY: Bell Tower, 2002.

Stiles, Mukunda, as Interpreted by. *Yoga Sutras of Patanjali,* San Francisco, CA/ Newburyport, MA: Weiser Books, 2002.

Acknowledgements

I would like to thank the following people for helping me with this book. Their suggestions were invaluable.

My dear wife Nancy – editor and English teacher assisted in proofreading.

My wonderful daughter Dr. Catherine E. Price – neuropsychologist and avid yoga practitioner gave advice on interior design, chapter headings and consistency of terms.

My close friend and cohort in awareness, Dr. James J. Barrell – author and psychologist helped to keep me on track concerning the authenticity and exactness of Patanjali's verses.

My dear friend and neighbor Gary Haskins – artist, potter, and poet provided suggestions on ways to improve many illustrations, font size, and verse numbering.

My dear friend Cejas Yogi (Tobe Terrell) who is always a spiritual guide and inspiration in humility.

My dear friend Yogi Madhvacarya (Michael Beloved) provided encouragement.

And last but not least, Vishak Srinivasan, helped with Sanskrit translation and interpretation.

About the Author

Neil Crenshaw has been a practitioner and teacher of traditional yoga for over twenty years. He does *āsana* primarily to keep his body as limber as possible for sitting in meditation. His motto is, "If it hurts, don't do it." His other book relating to yoga is *You Can Develop Pure Awareness*.

Made in the USA
Coppell, TX
29 April 2022